Wildlife in the Rockies

Coloring Book

Copyright © 2012 Deborah S. Huffman

All rights reserved.

ISBN-13:978-1975714291

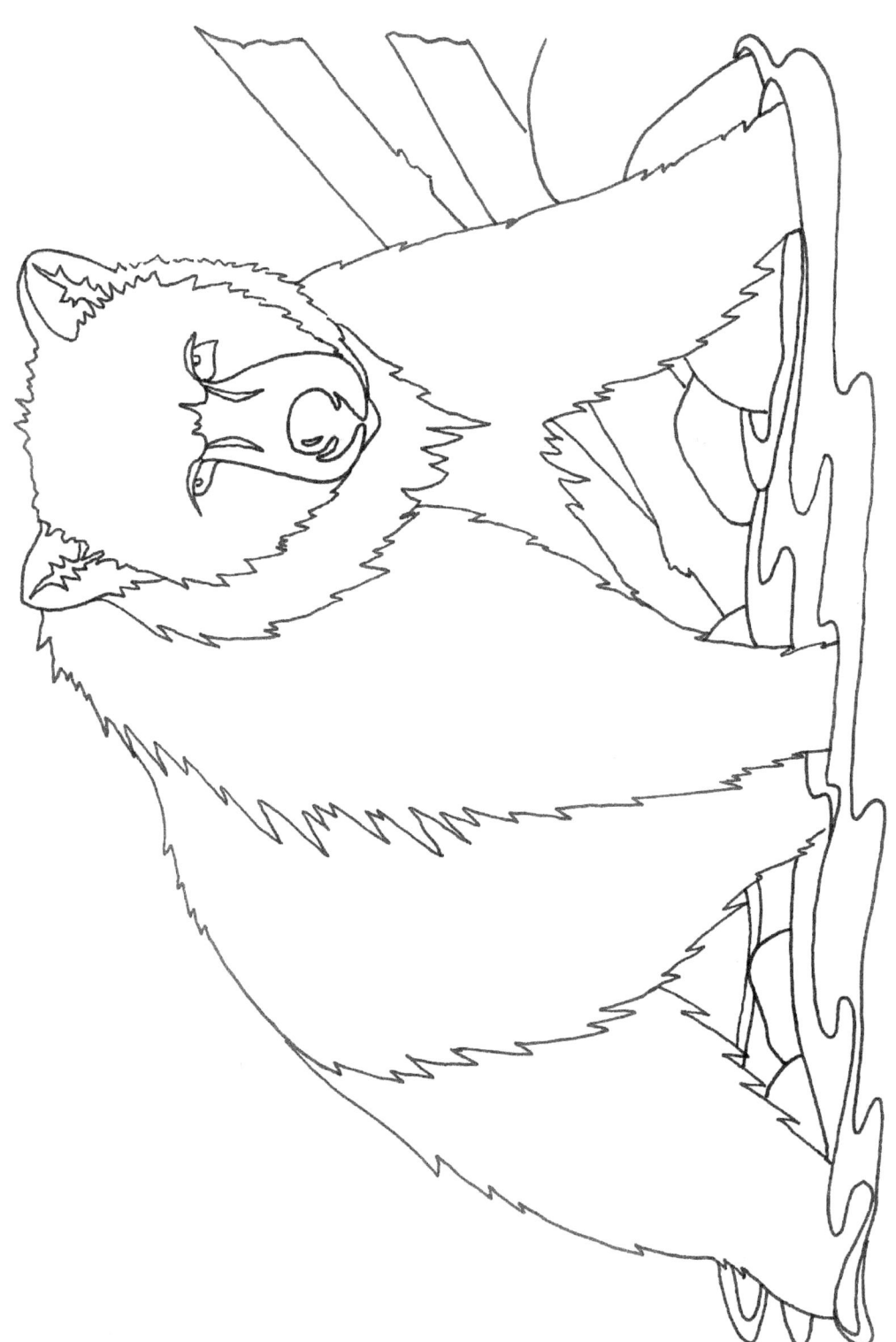

Water Bear

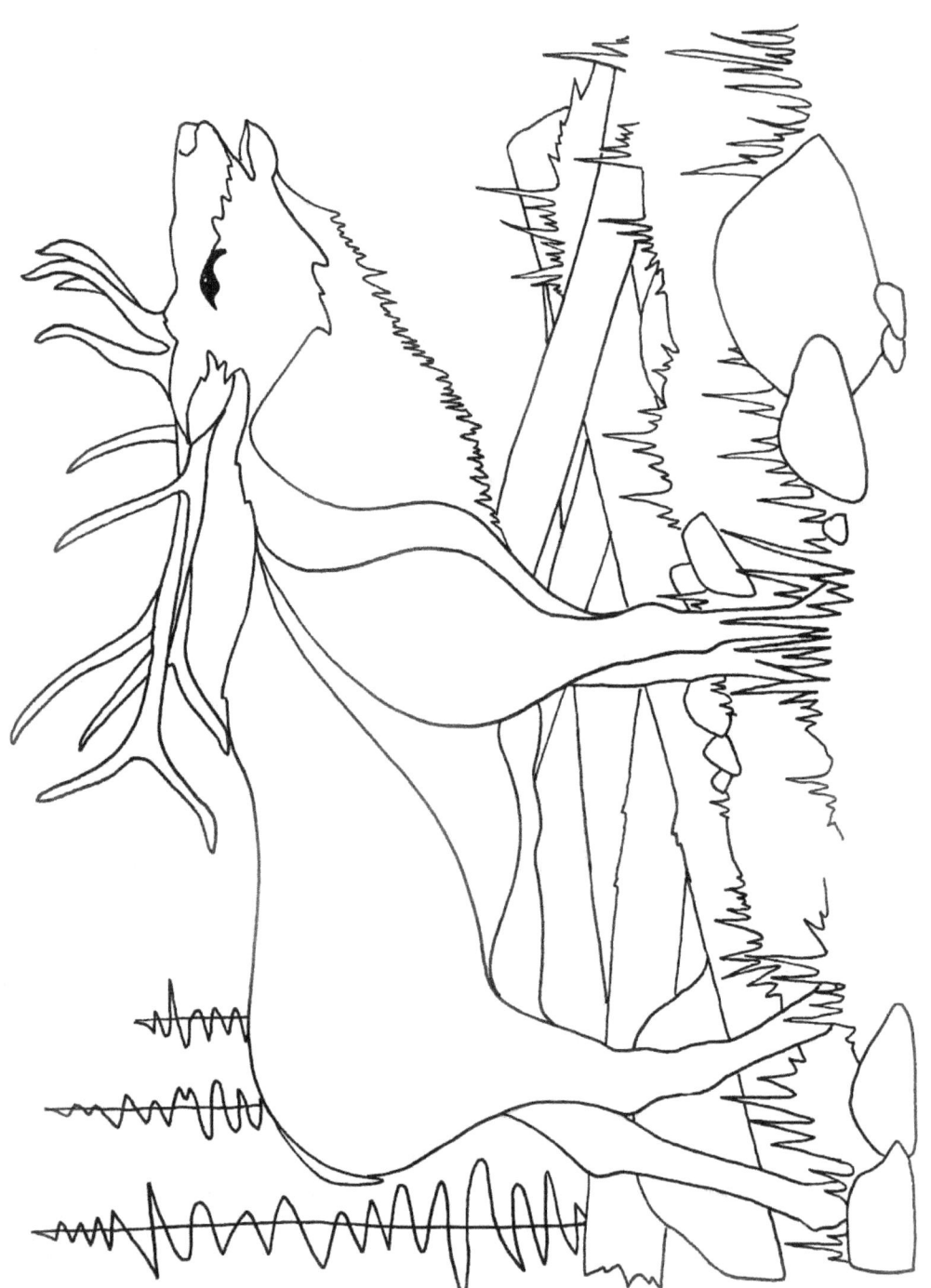

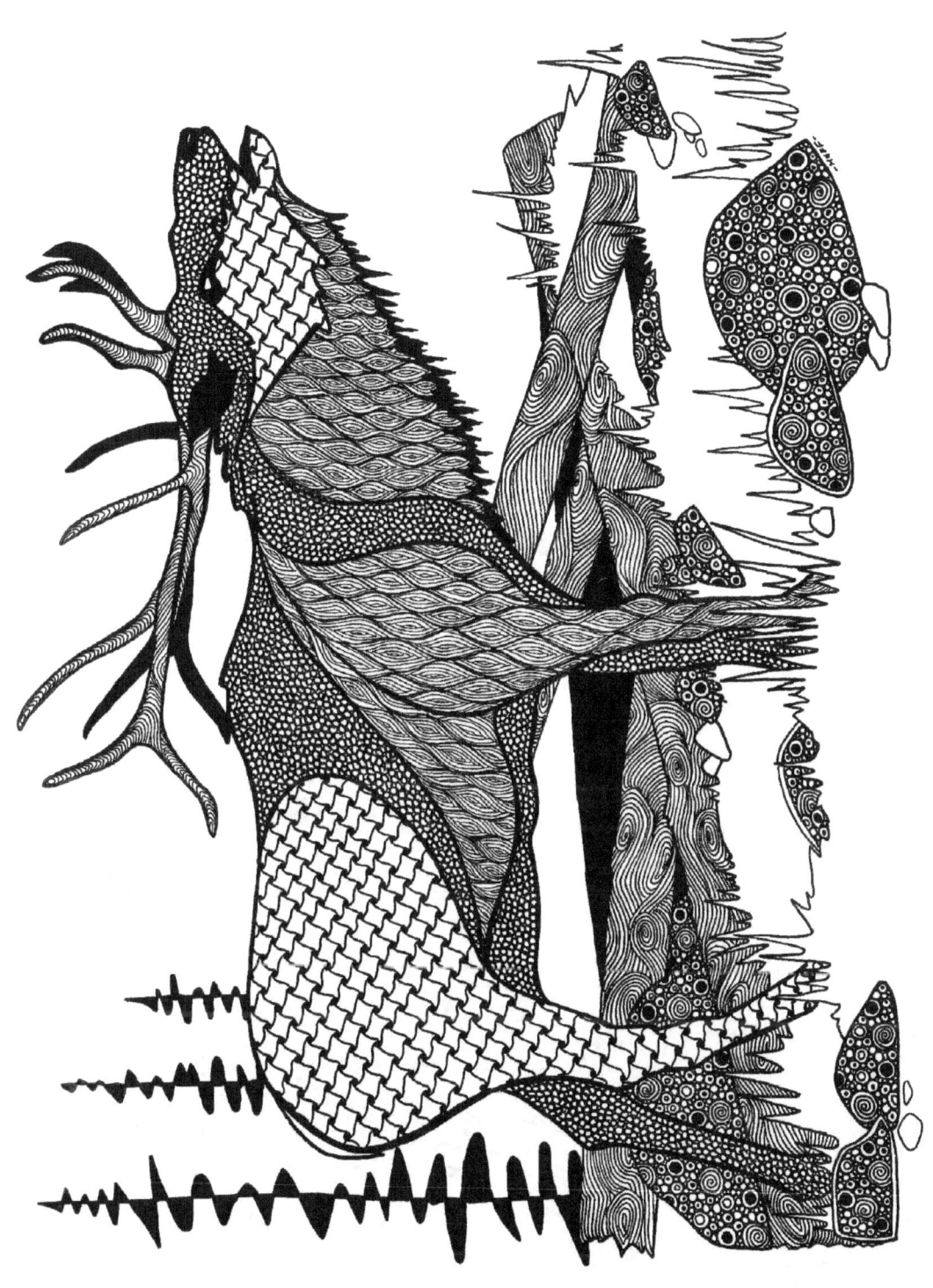

Bugling Elk

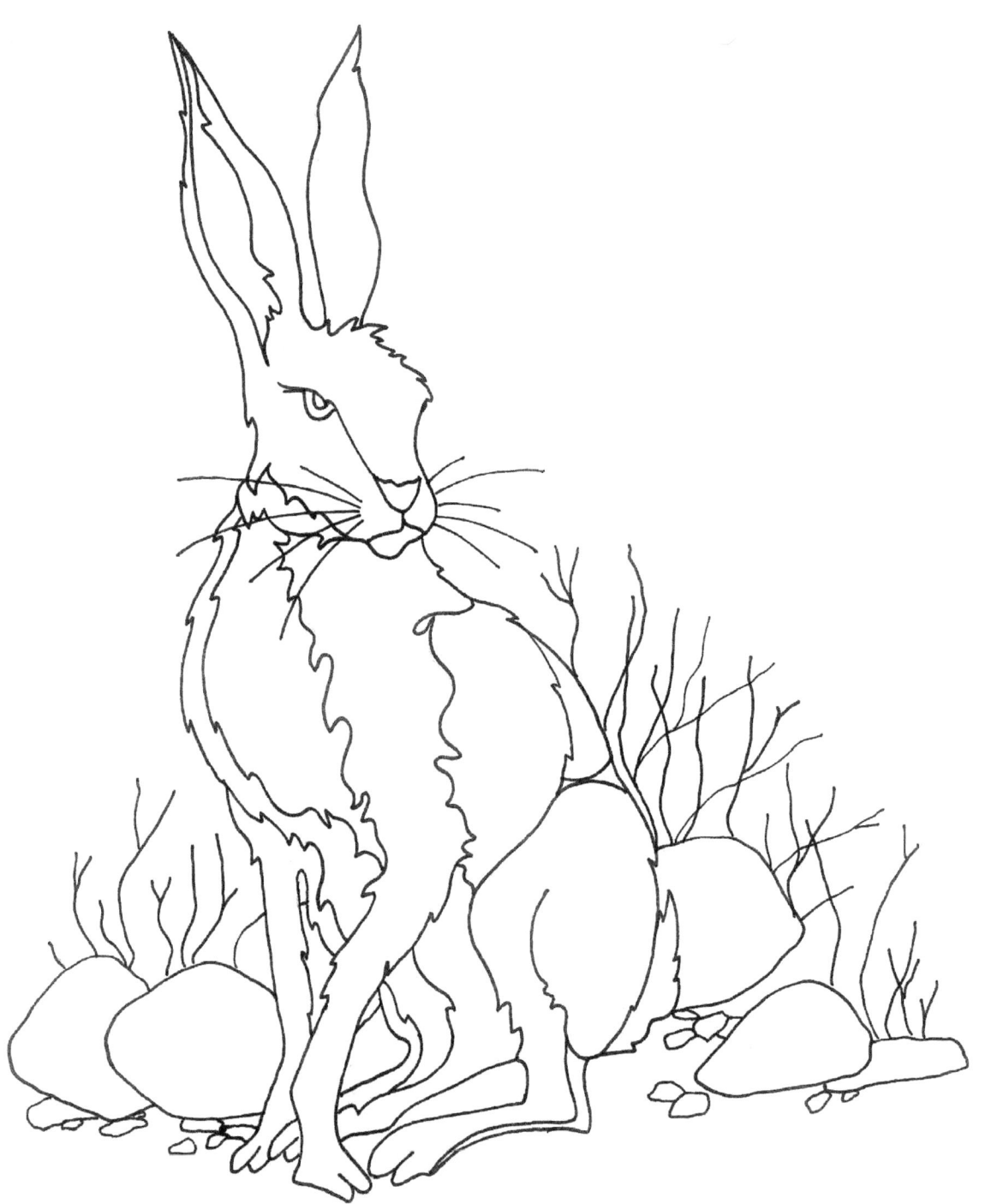

Sassy Jack Rabbit

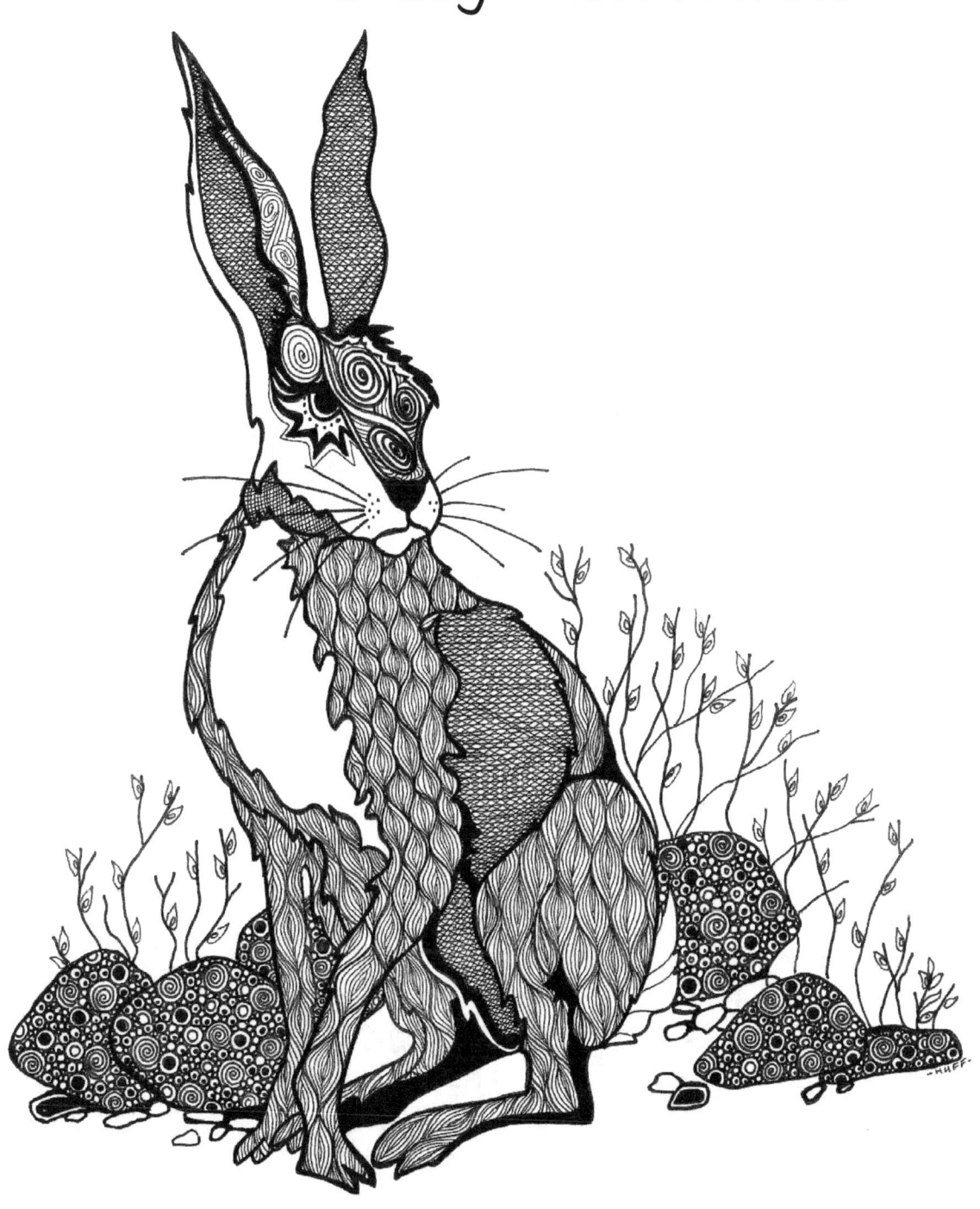

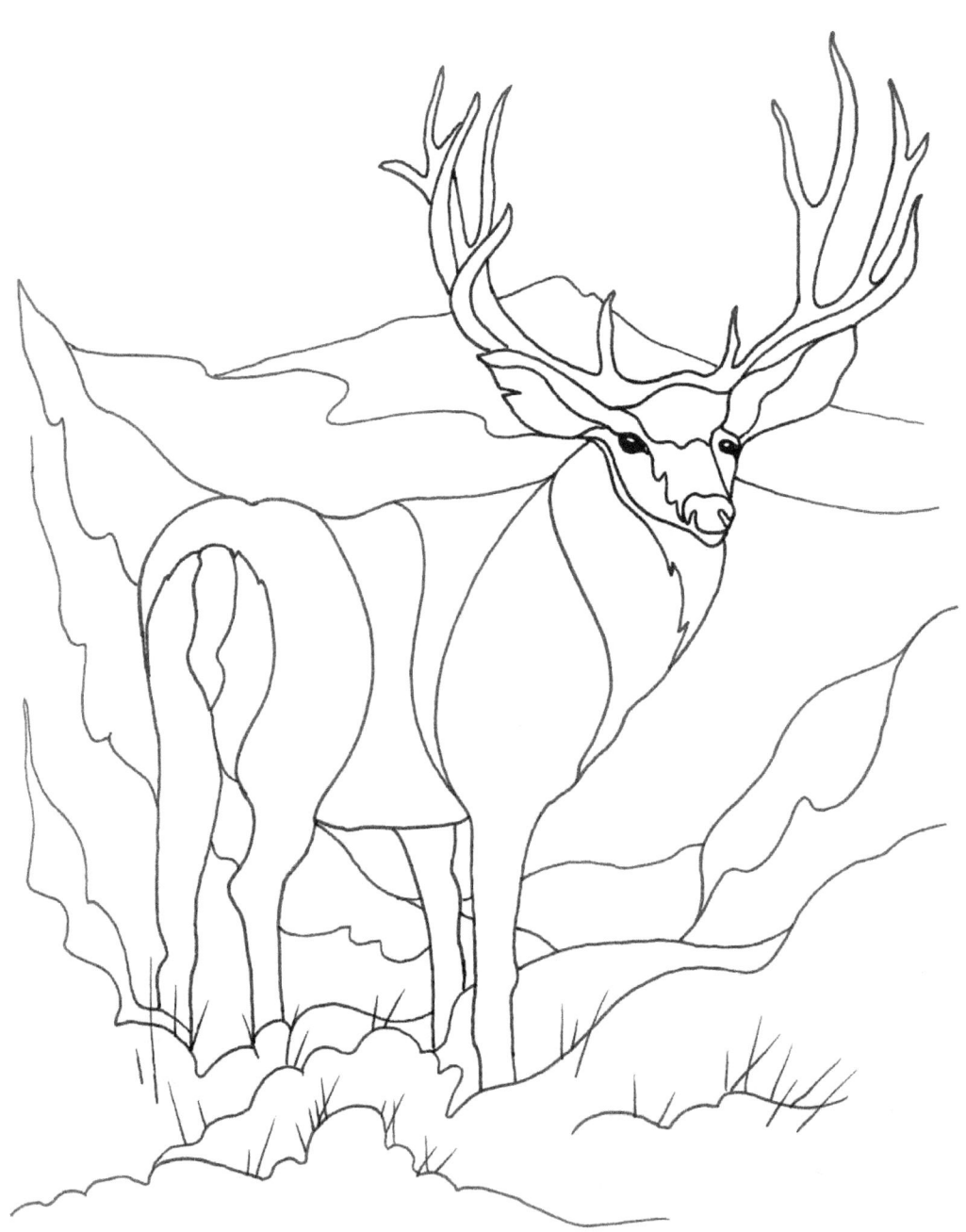

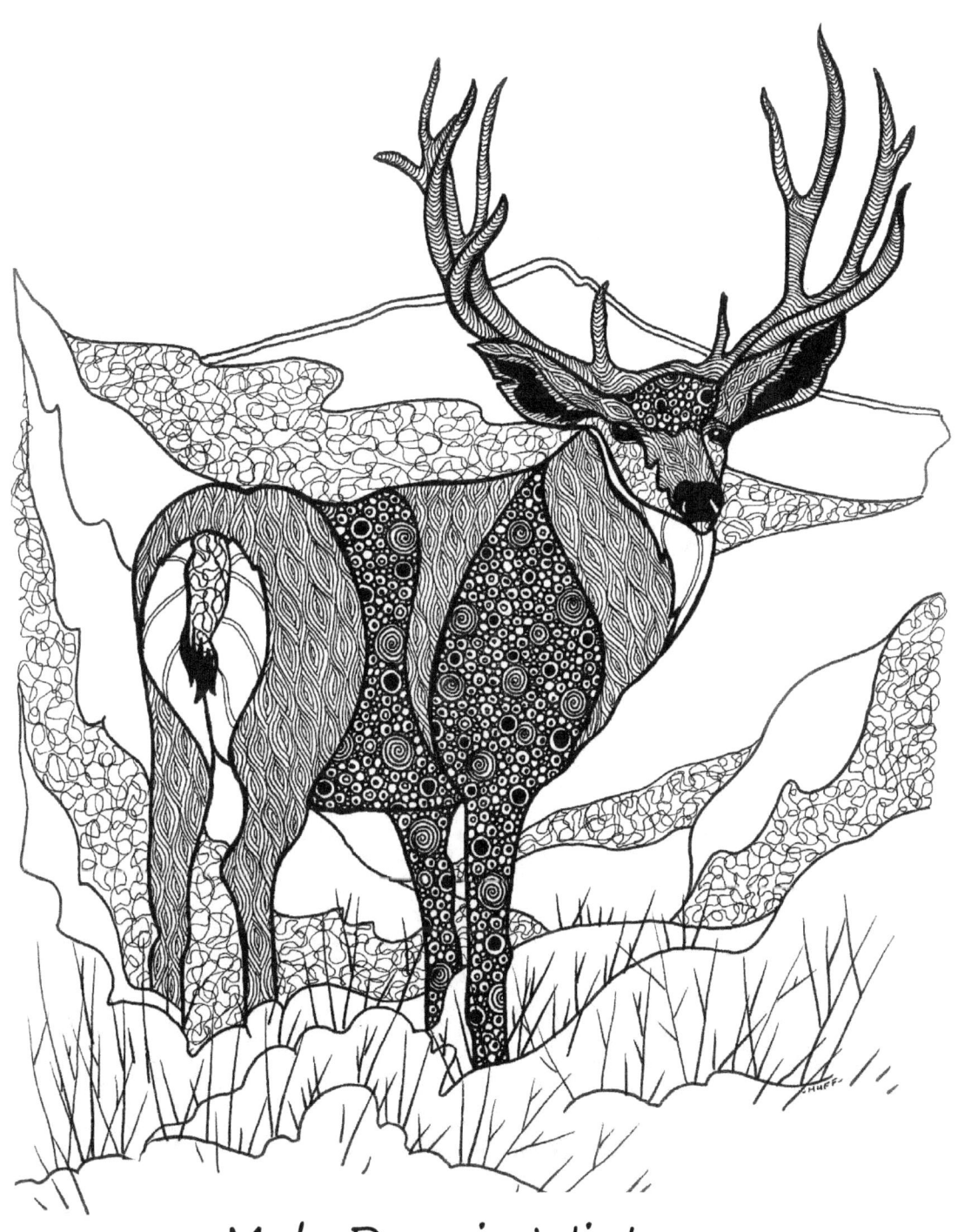

Mule Deer in Winter

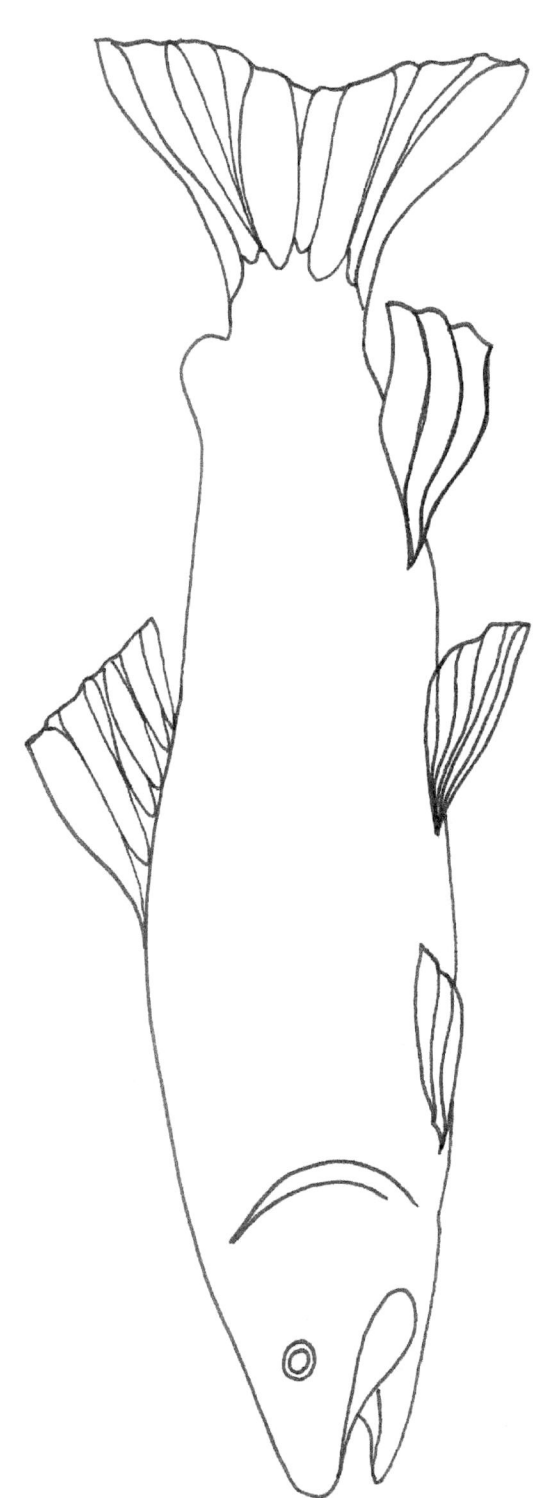

Dream Fish

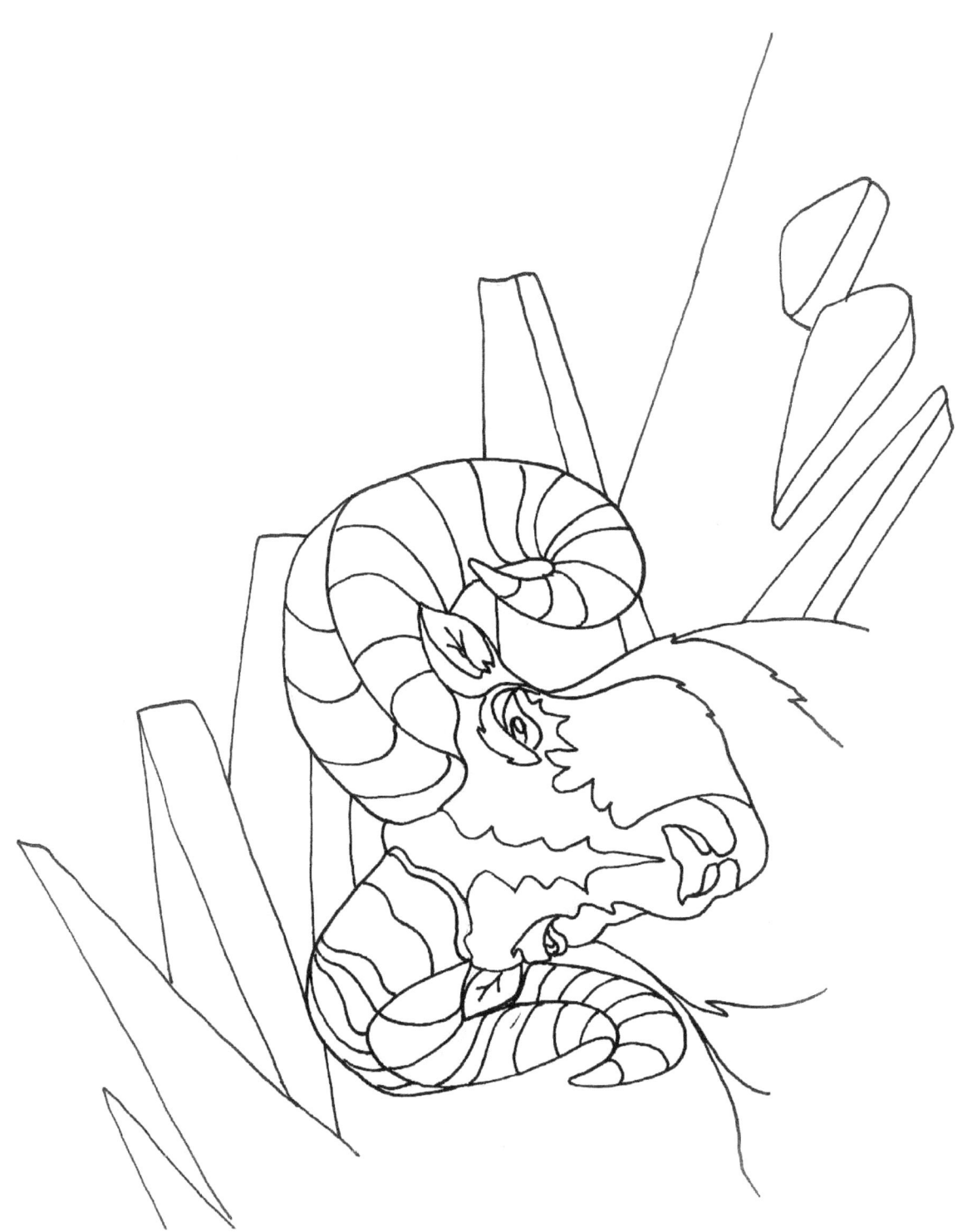

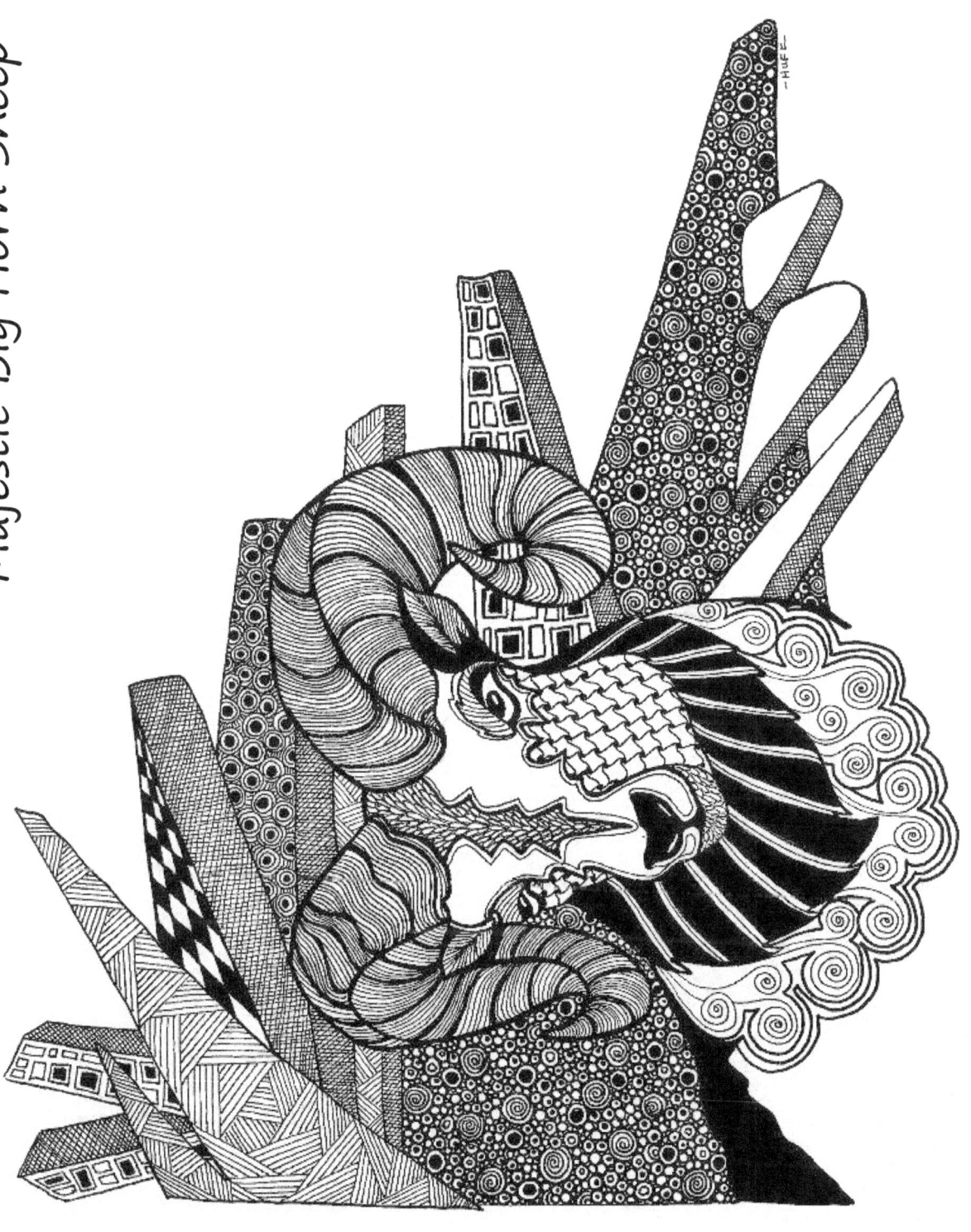

Majestic Big Horn Sheep

Pronghorn Antelope

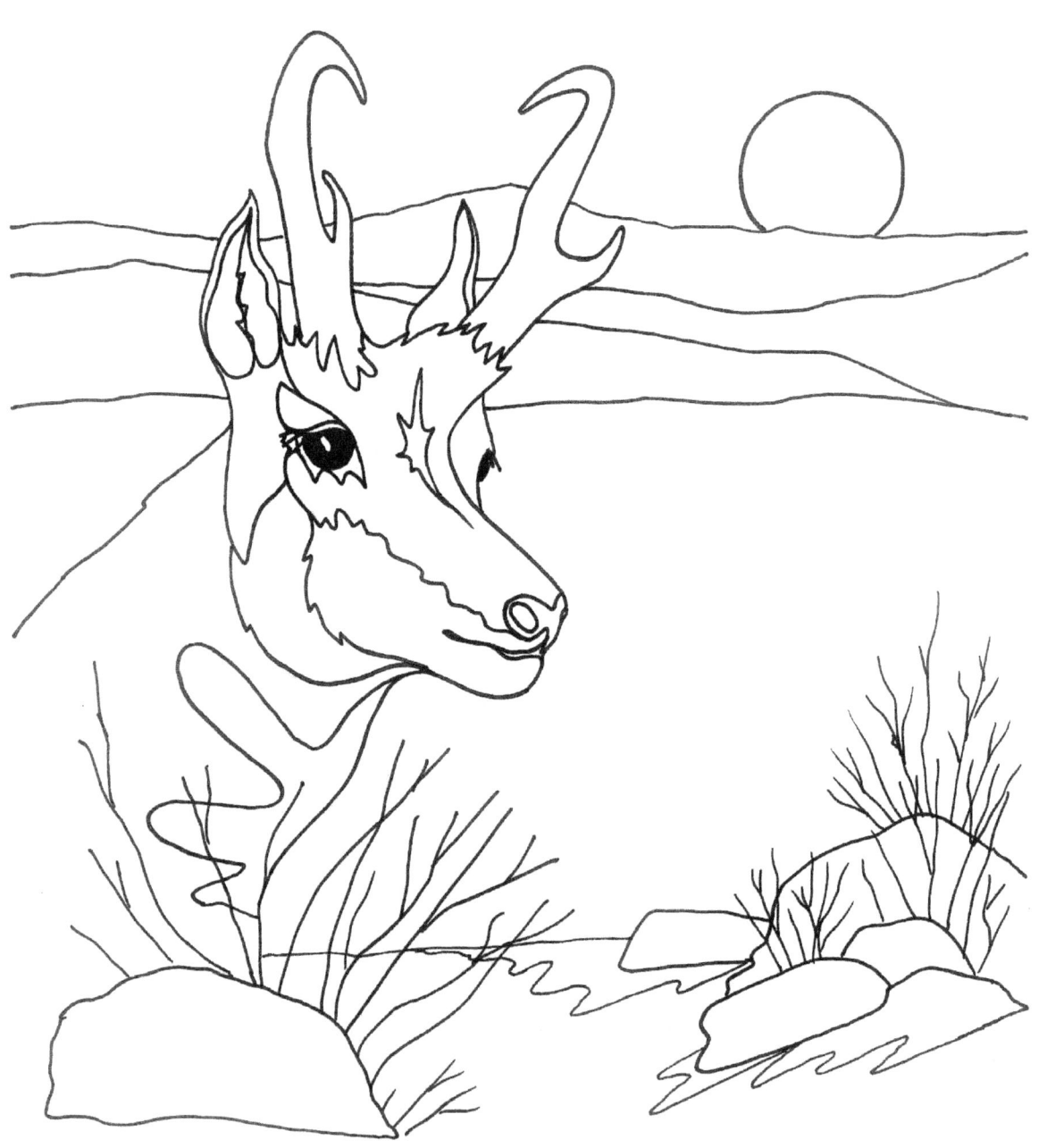

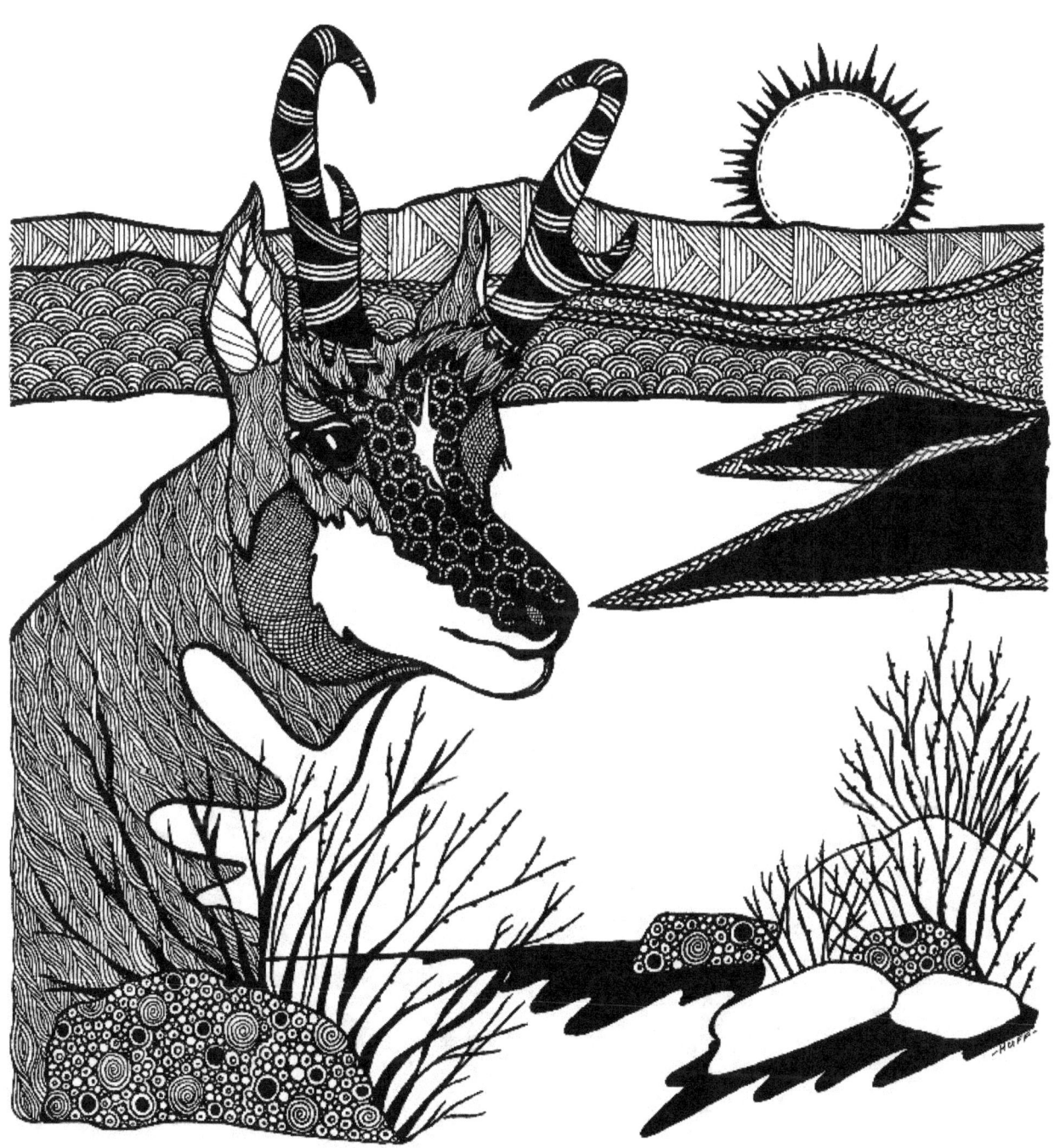

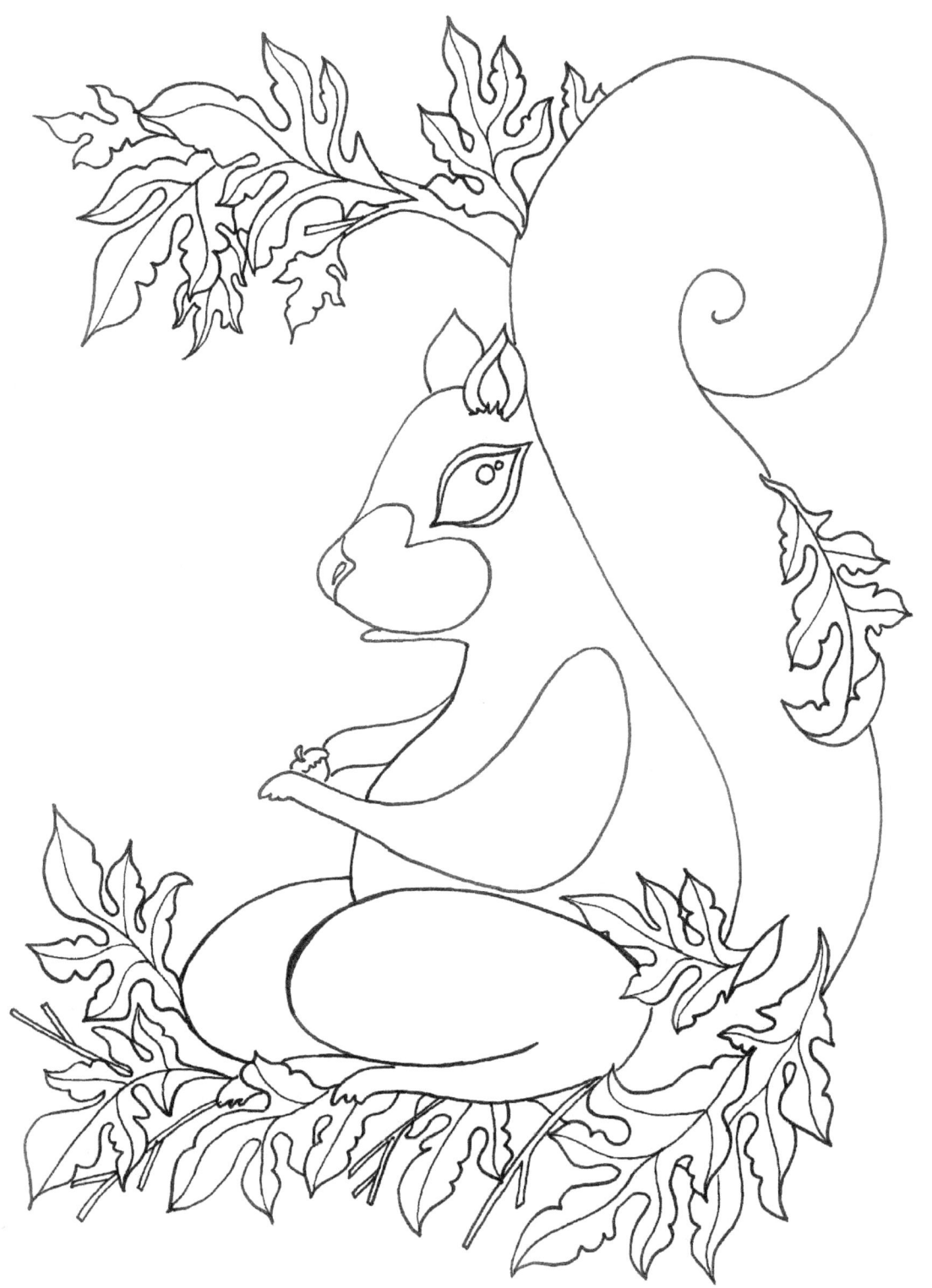

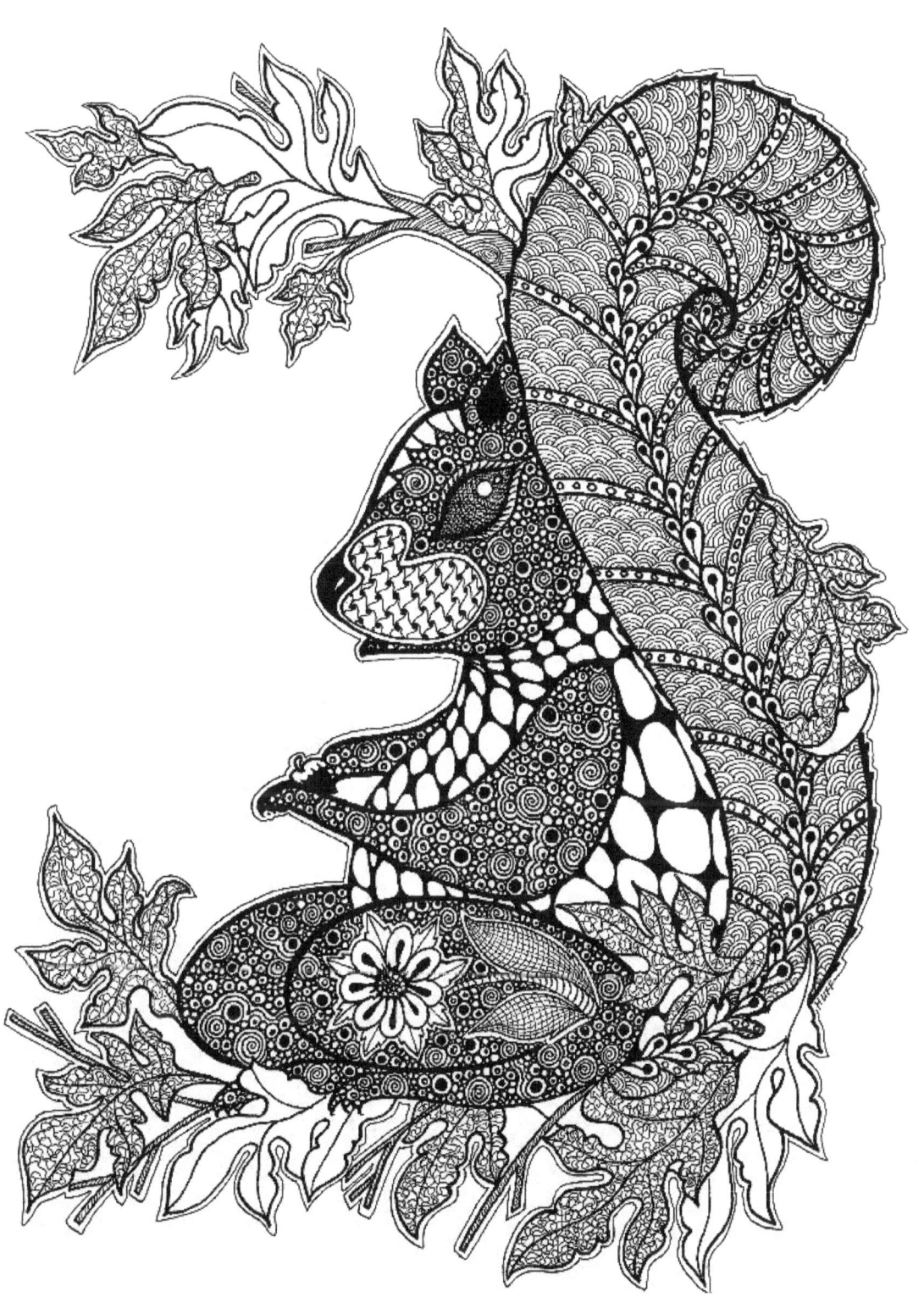

Squirrel perched on a limb

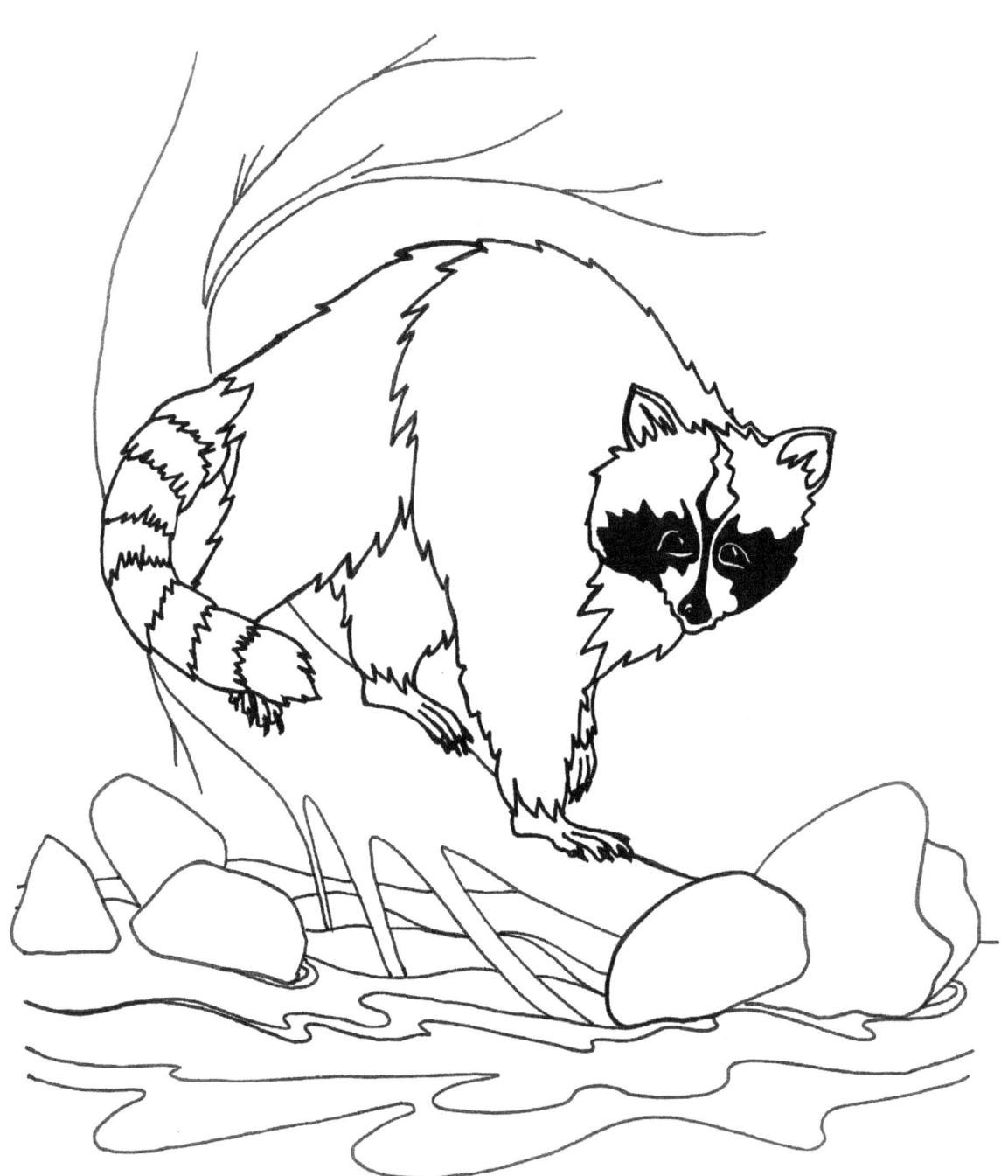

Raccoon

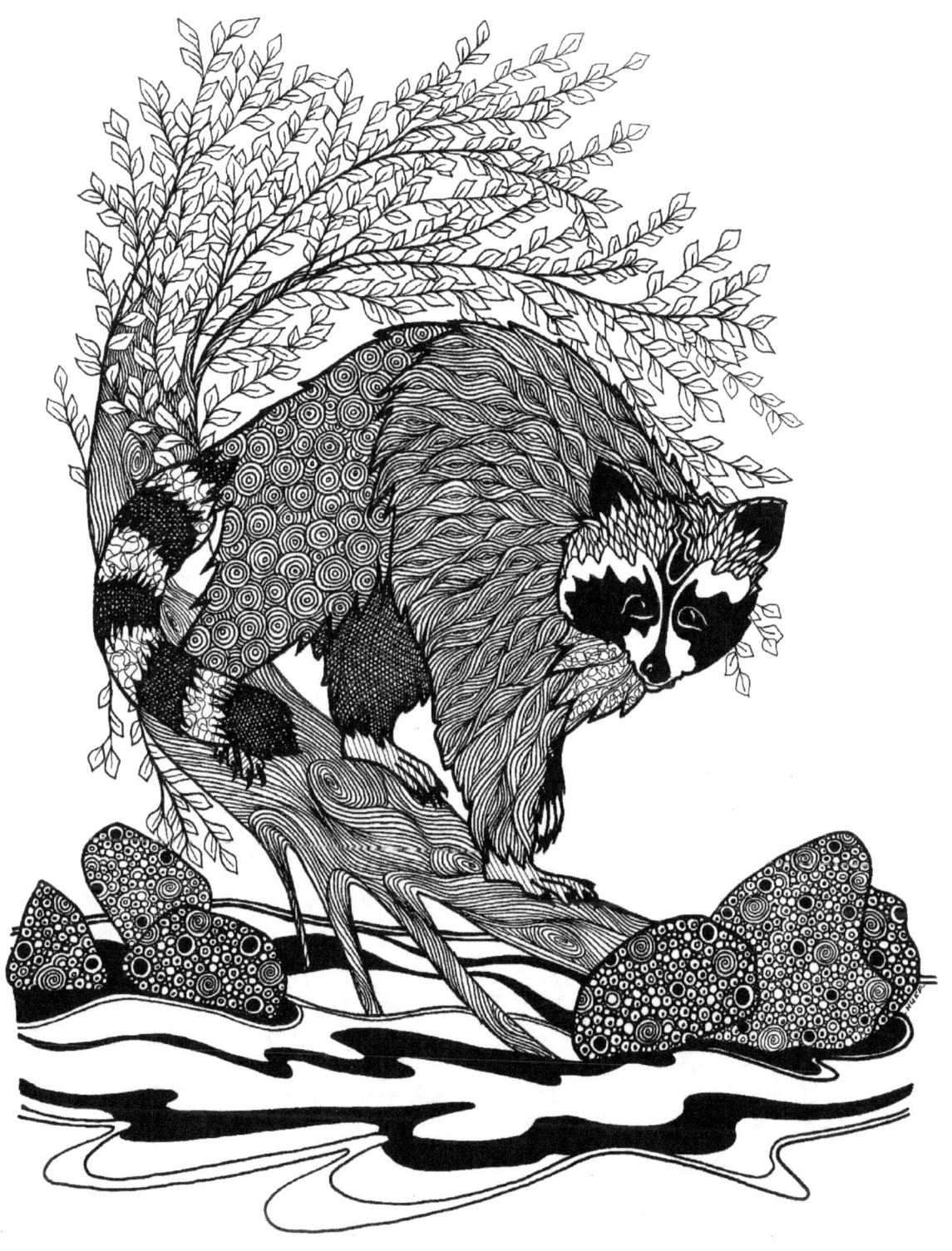

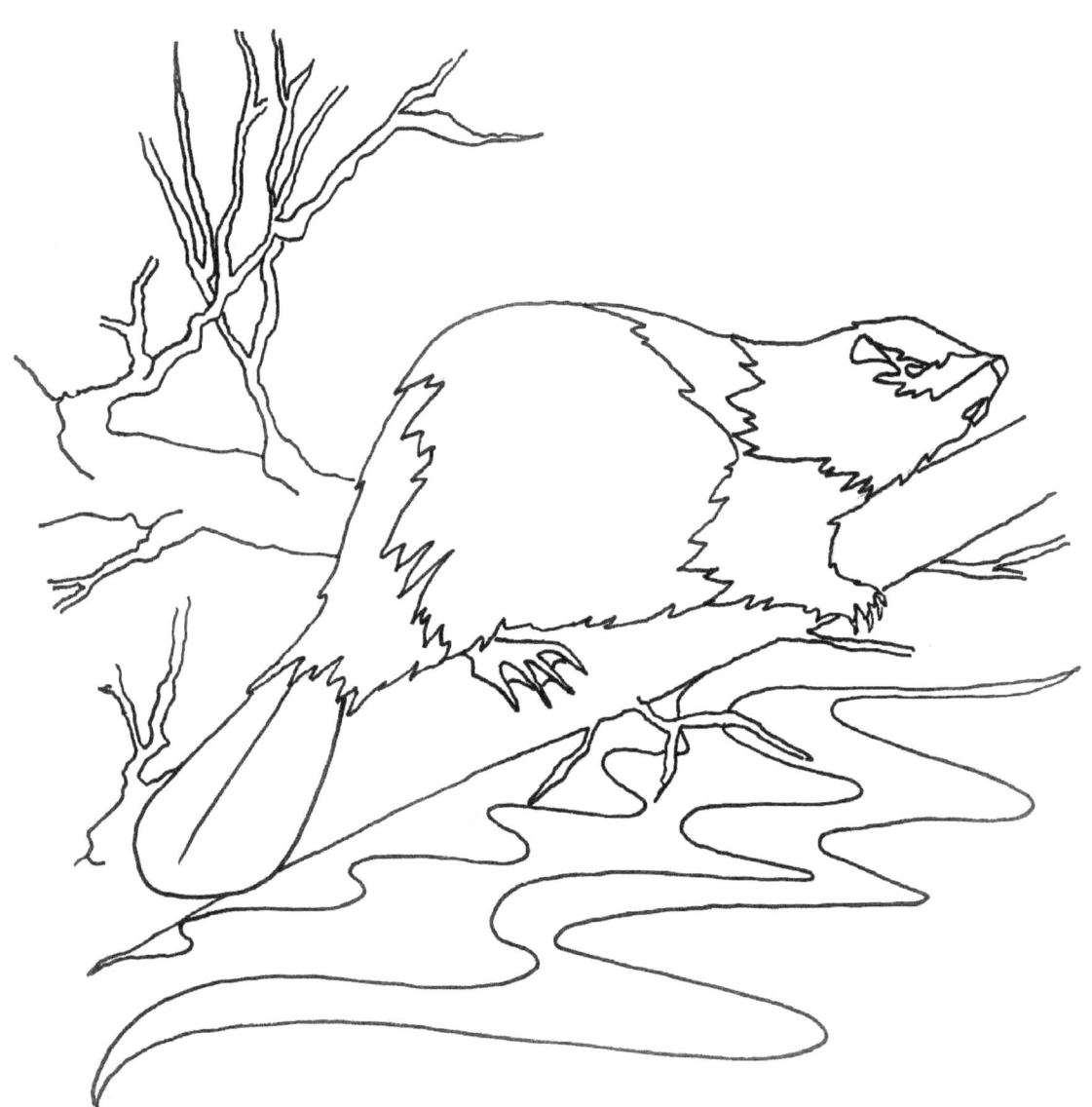

Beaver

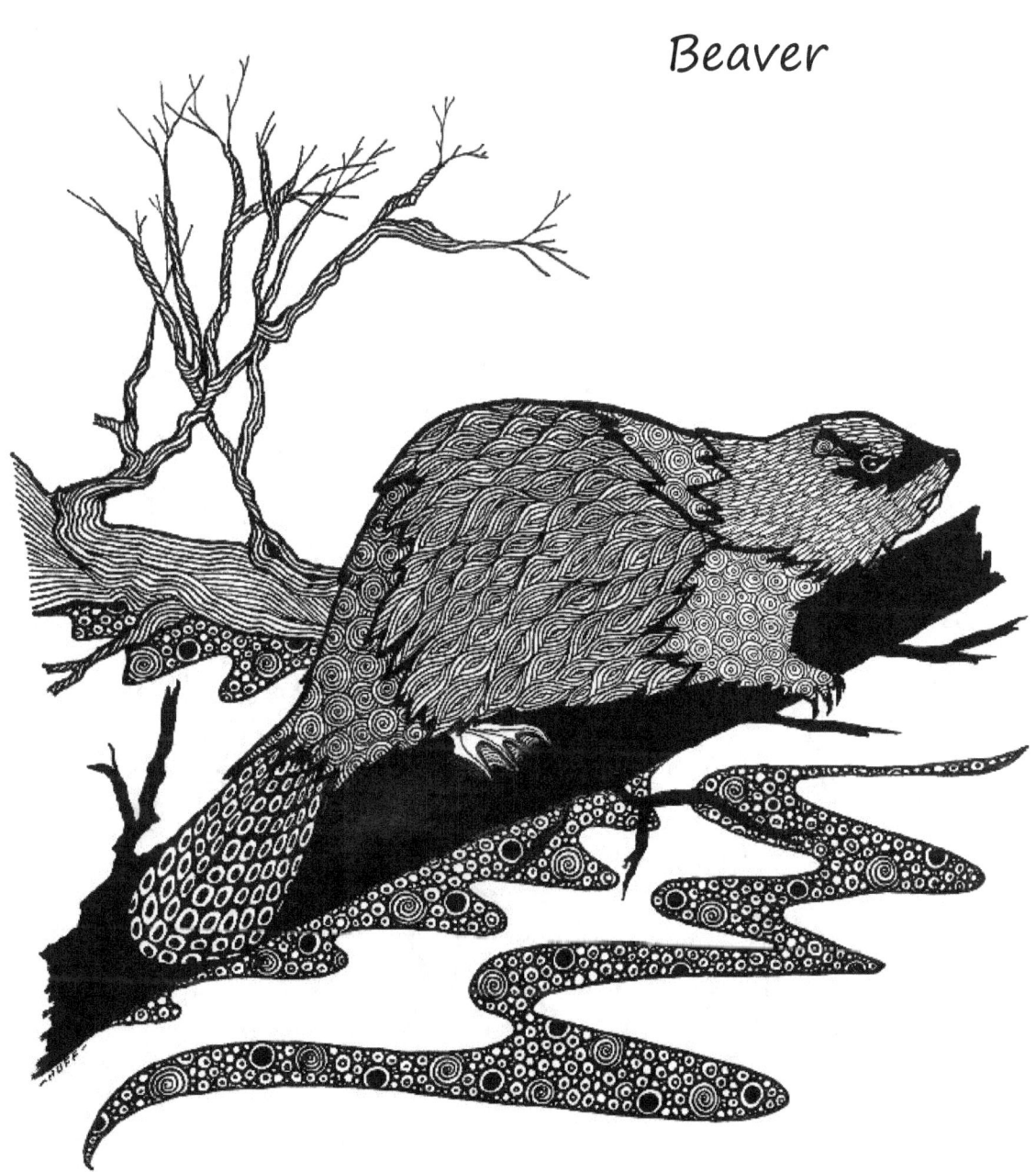

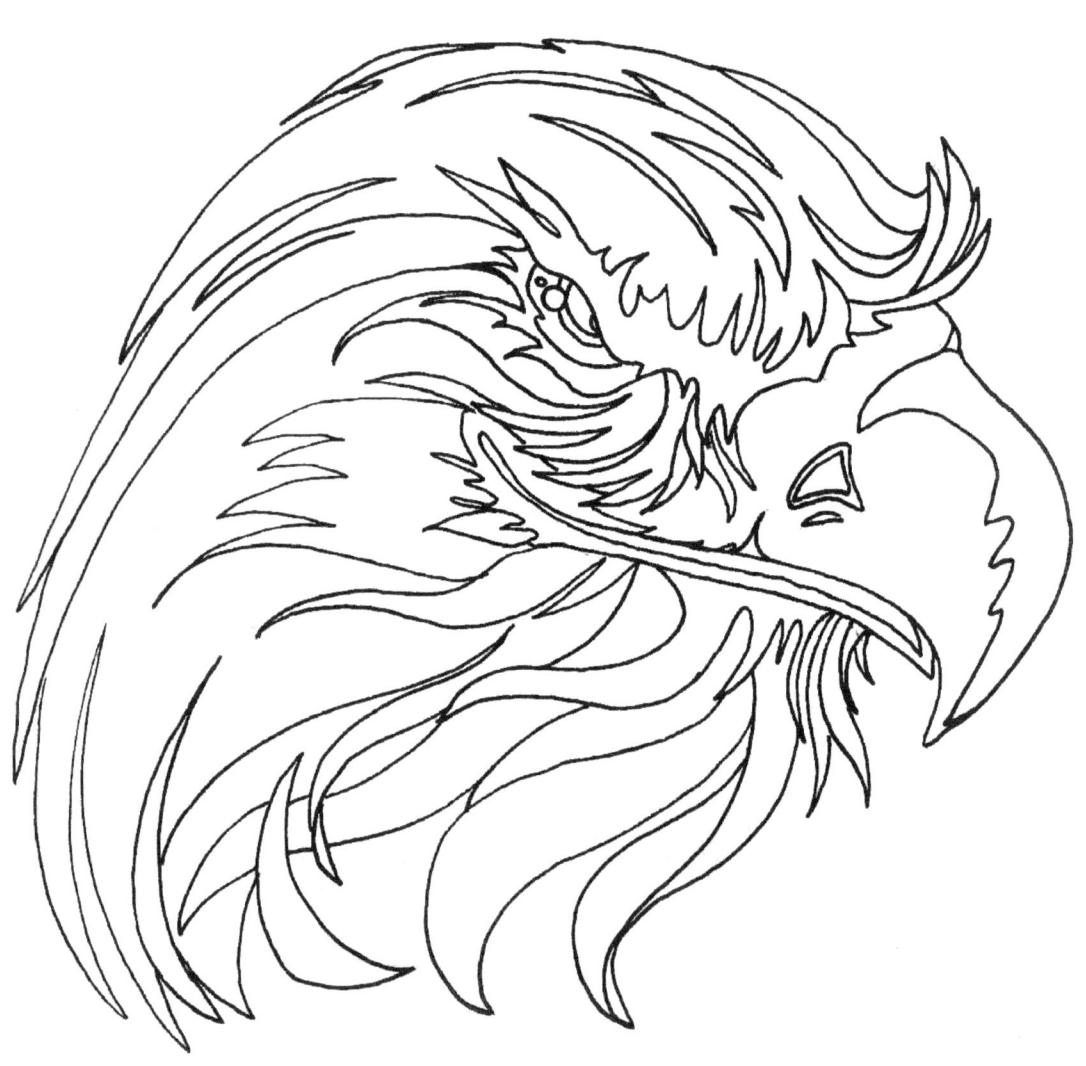

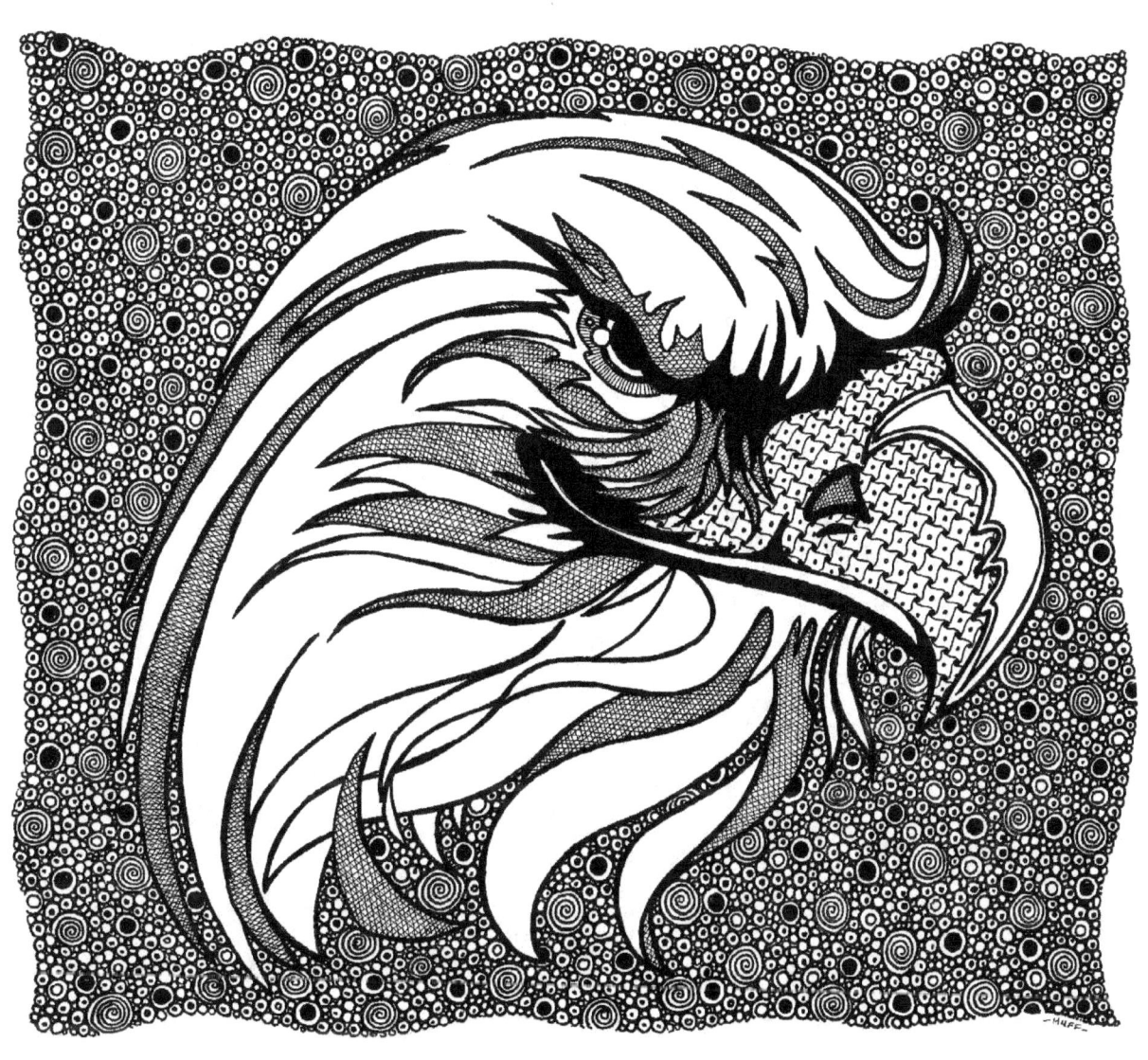

Bald Eagle

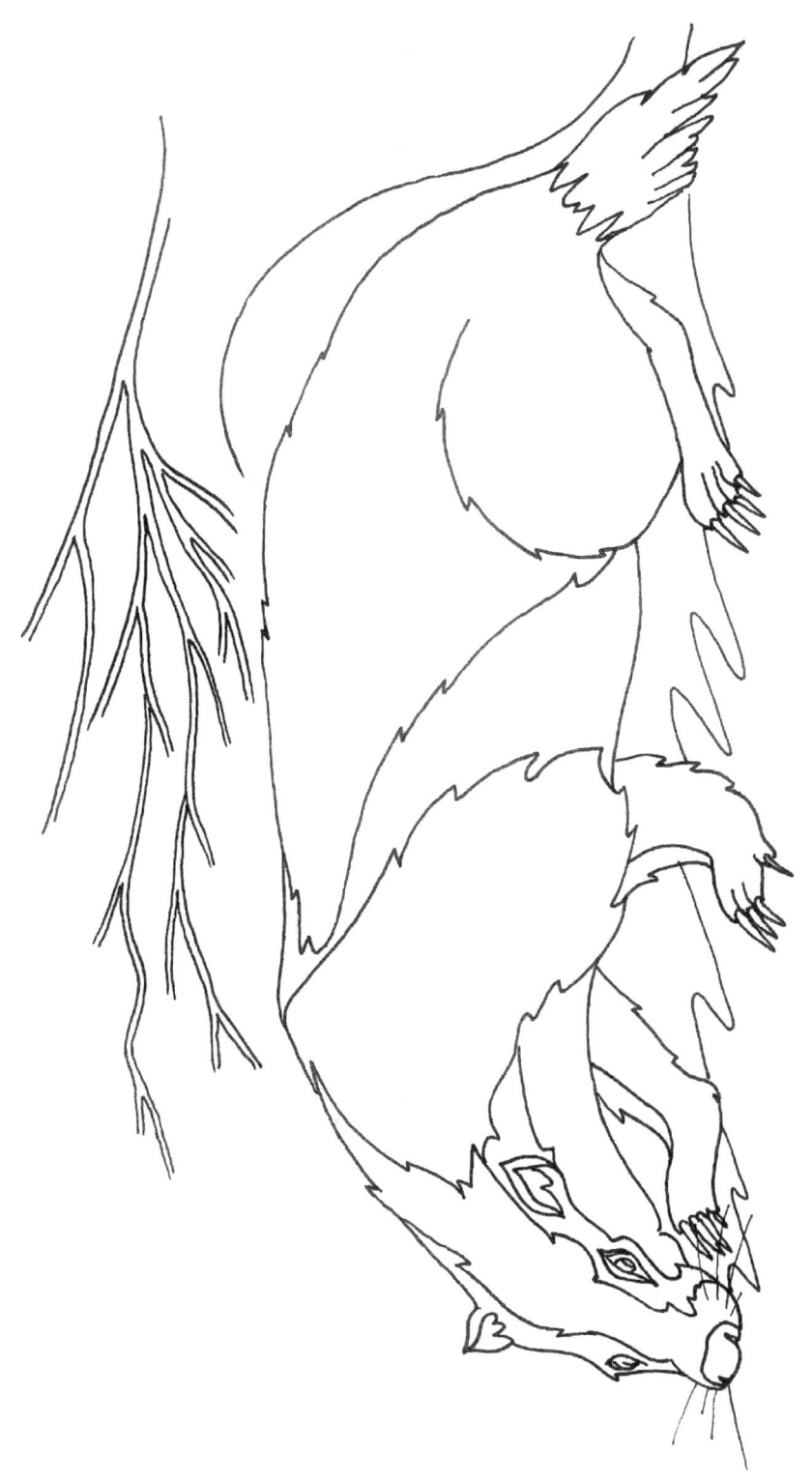

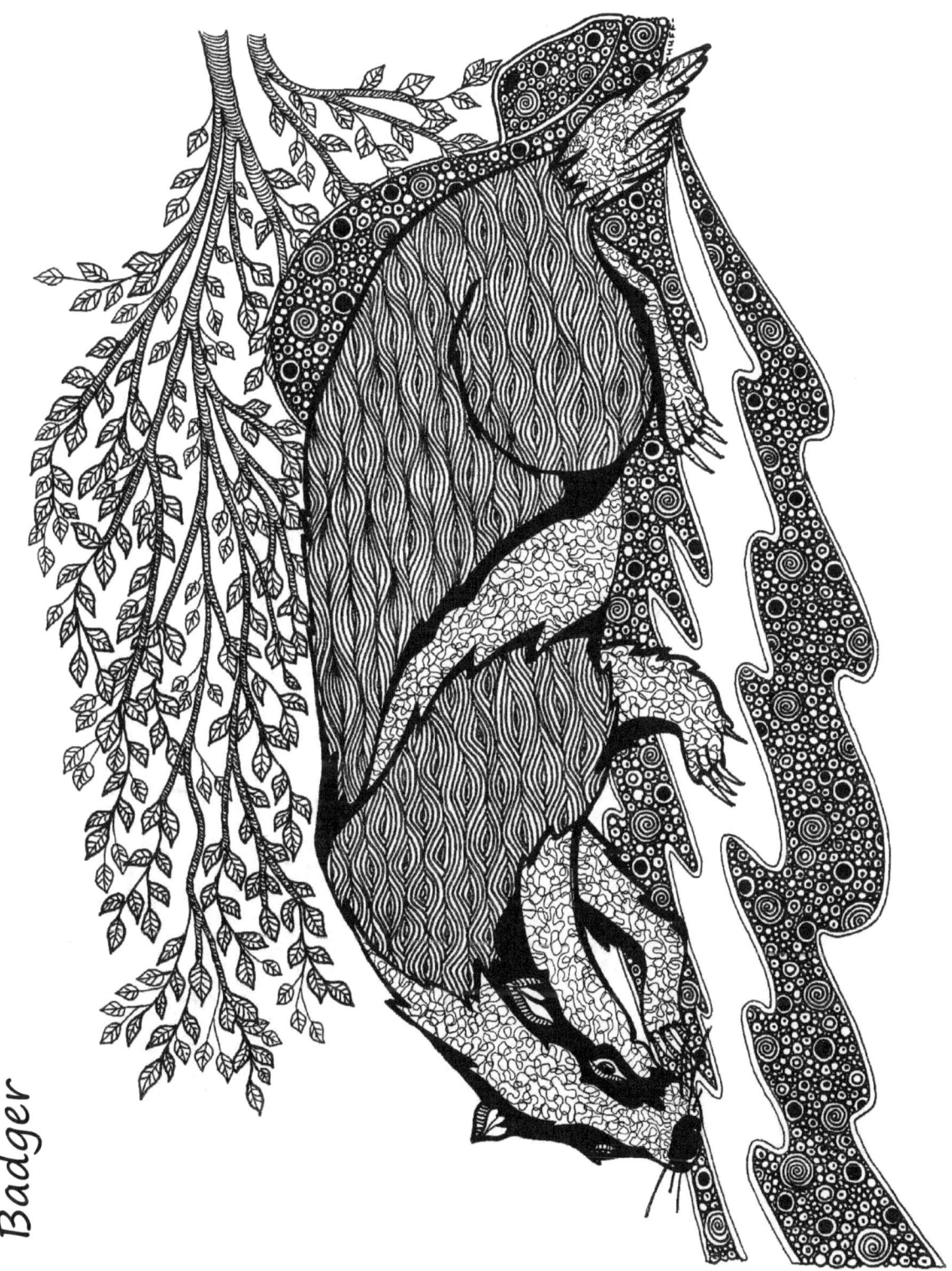

Badger

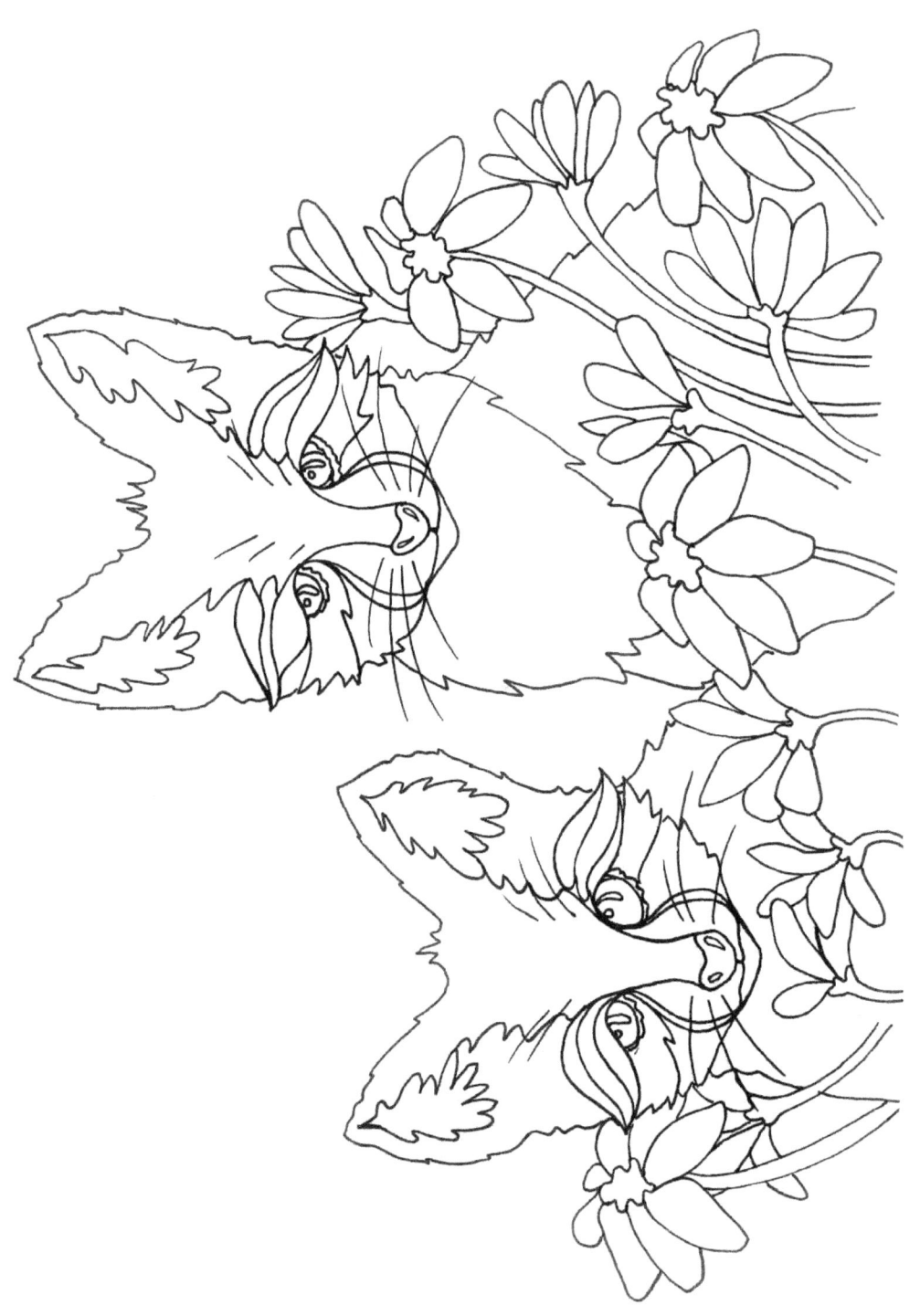

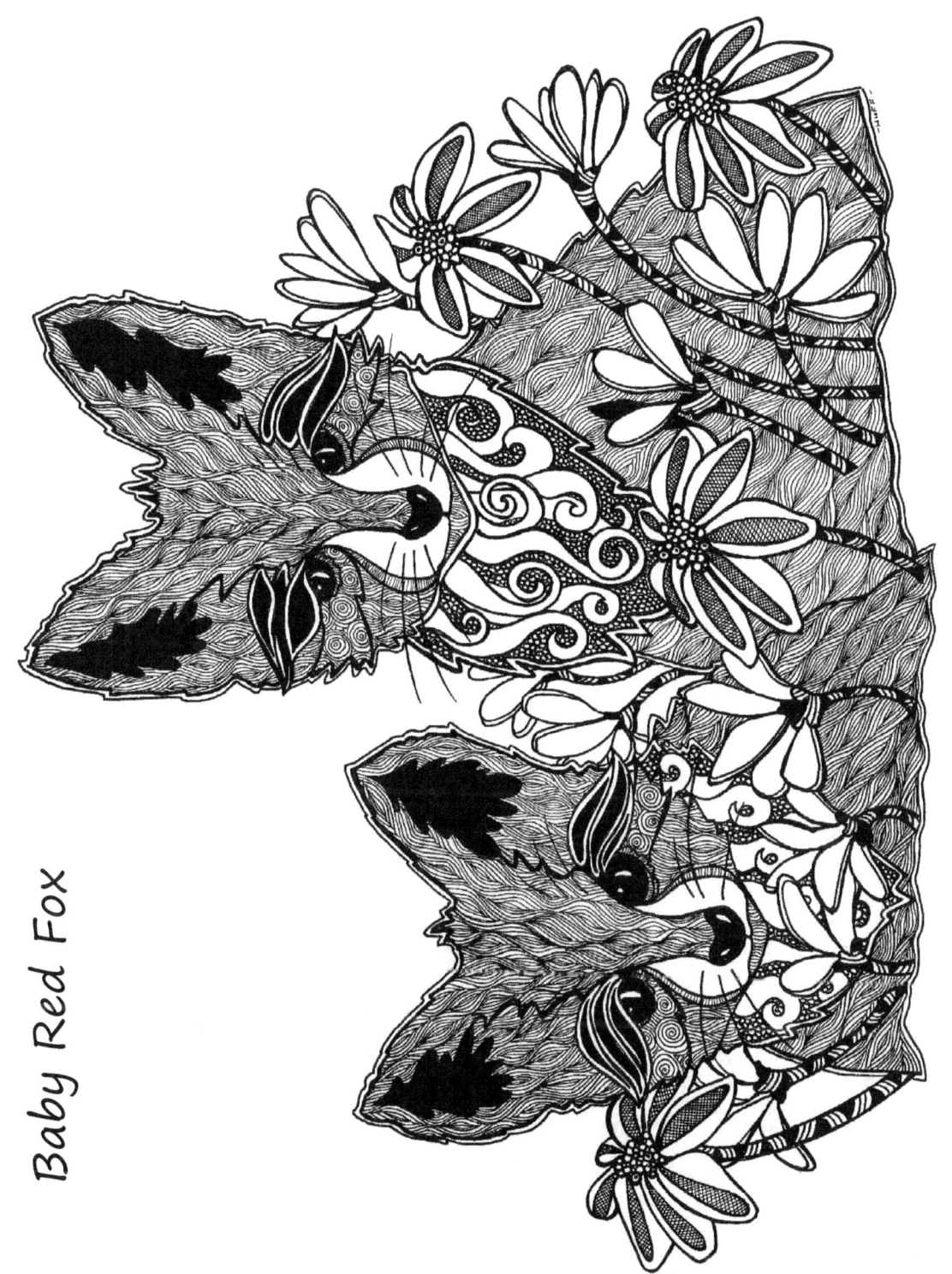

Baby Red Fox

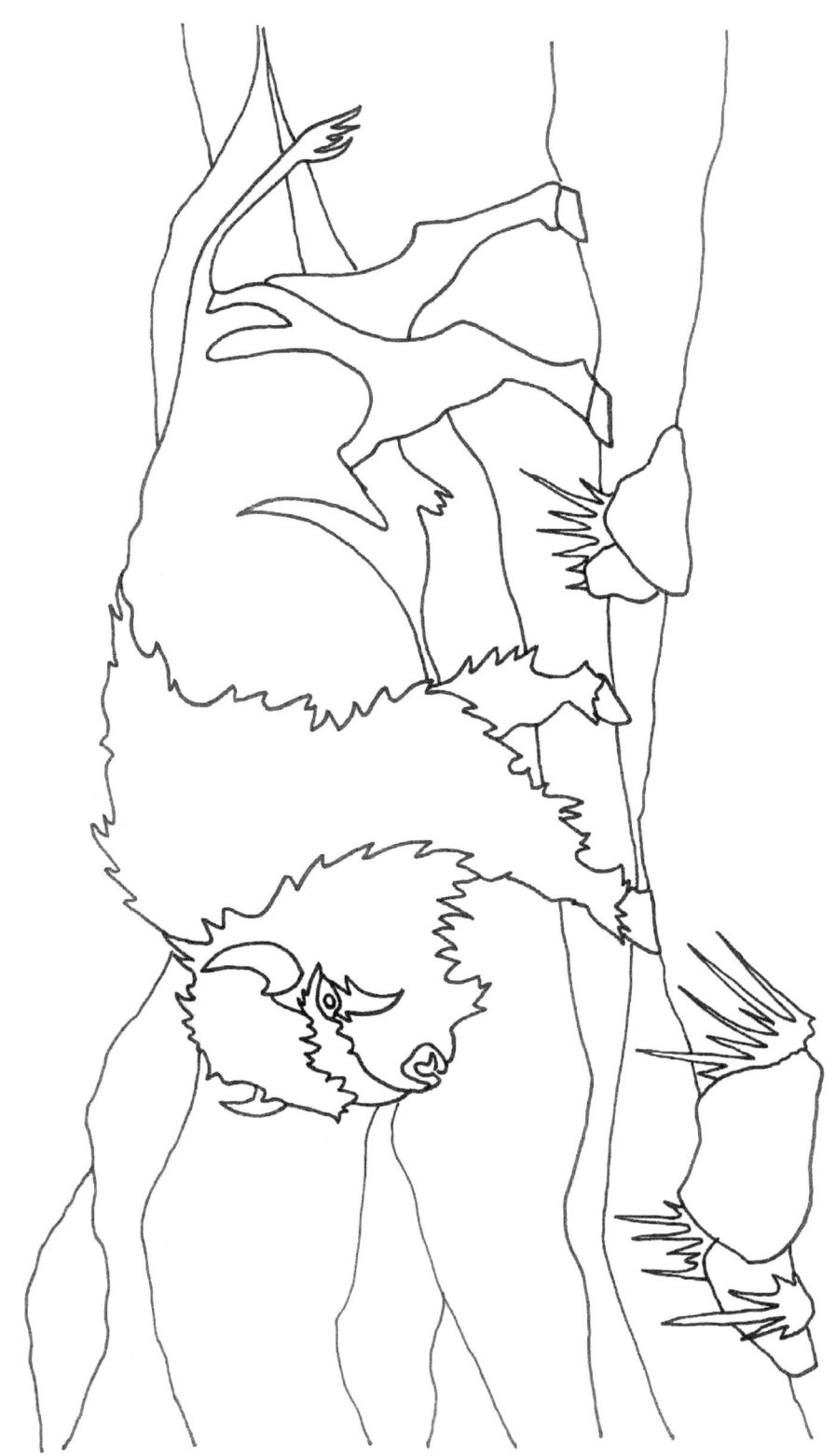

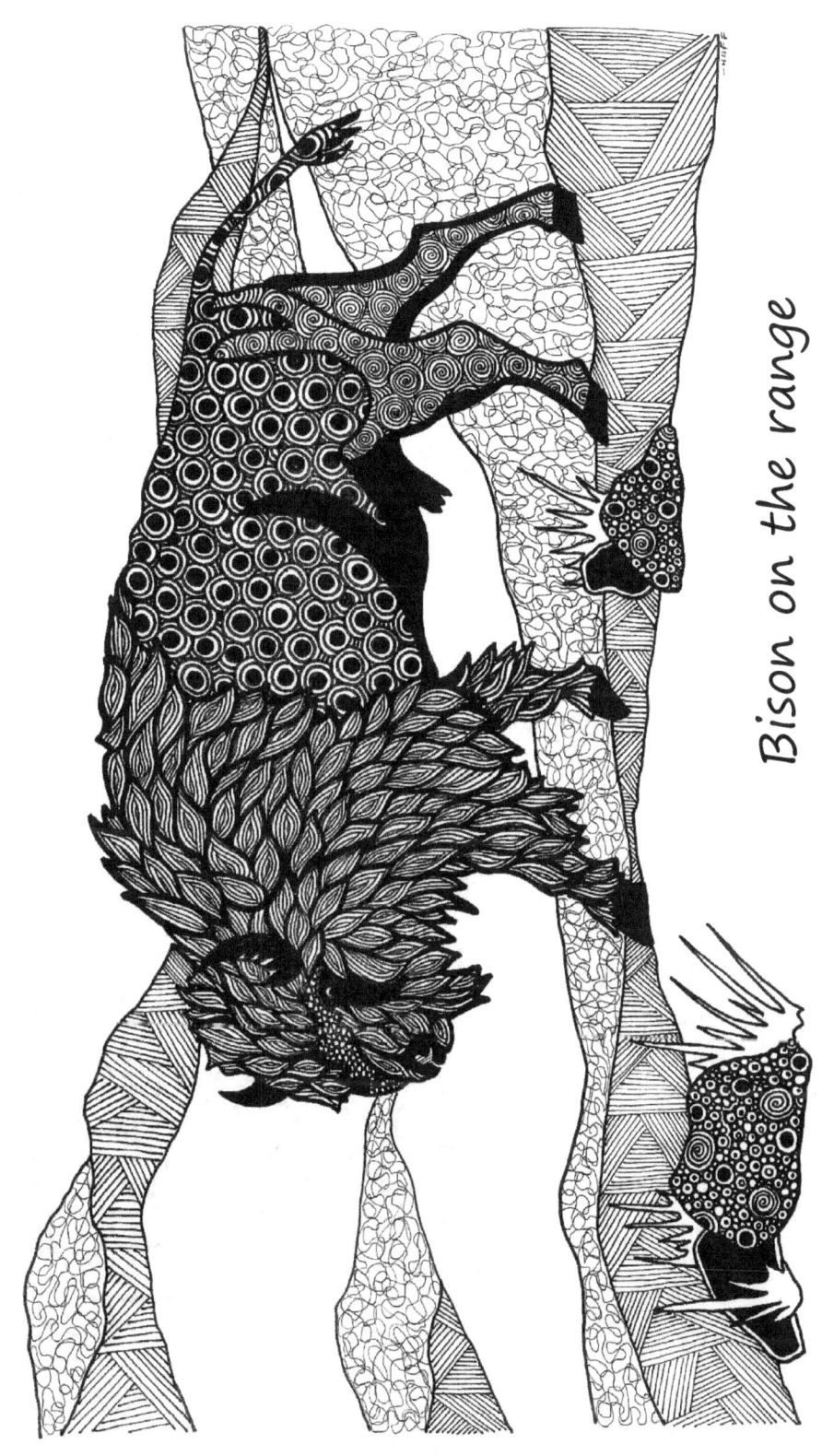

Bison on the range

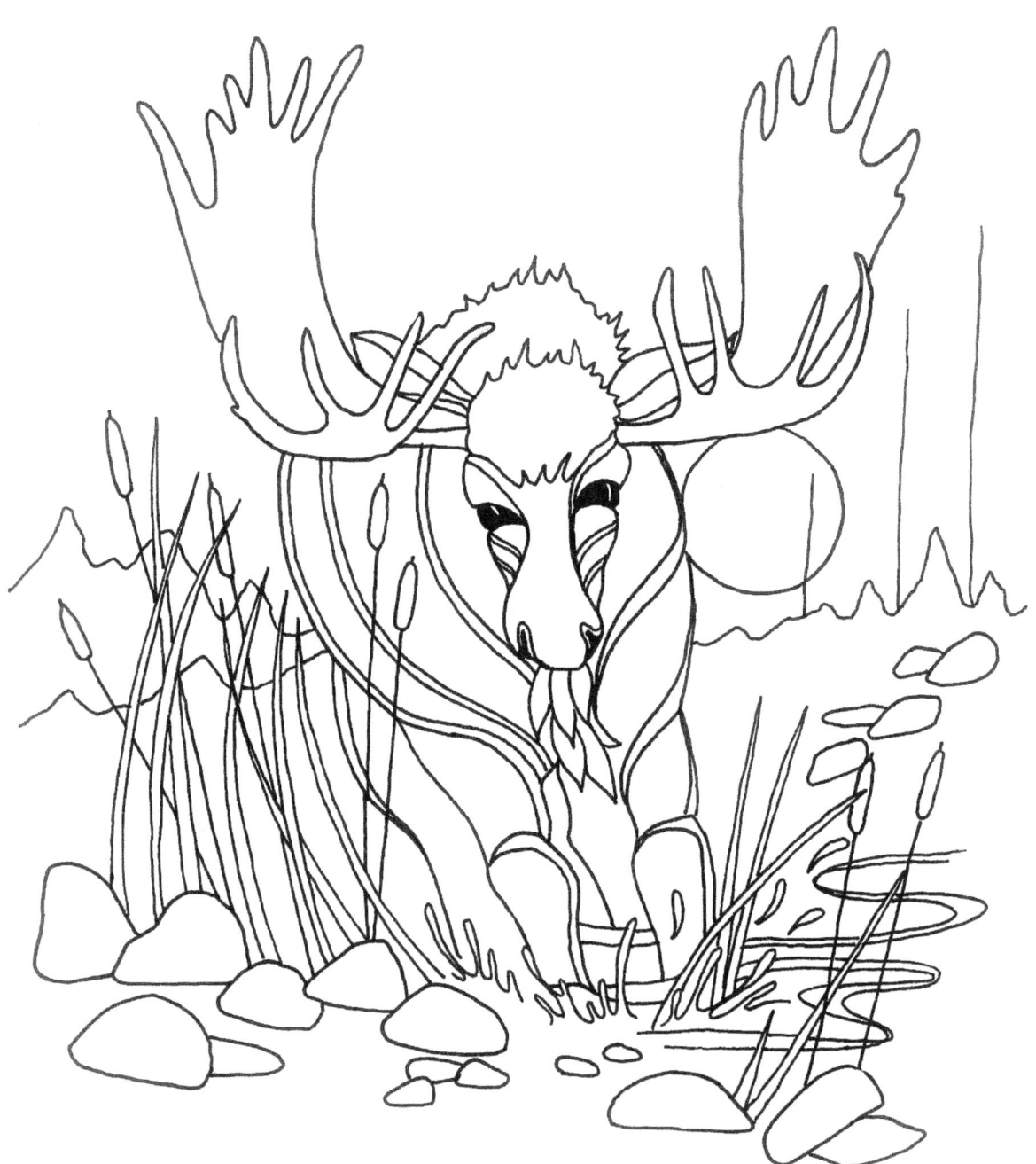

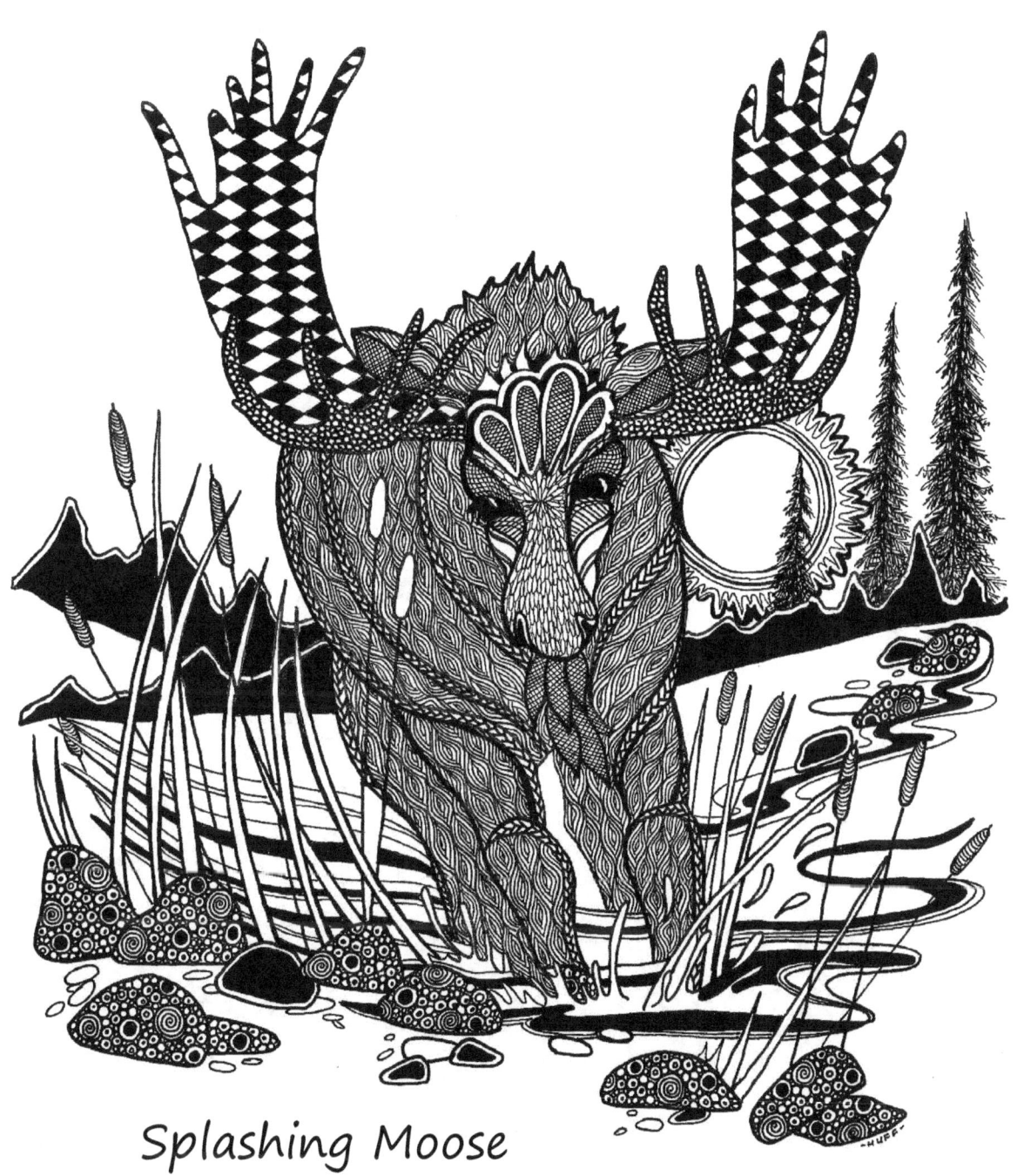
Splashing Moose

www.ingramcontent.com/pod-product-compliance
Lightning Source LLC
Chambersburg PA
CBHW062208220526
45470CB00009B/2975